What Is That?

Seed Learning

What is that?

That's a dog.

The dog
is barking.

What is that?

That's a fish.

The fish
is swimming.

What is that?

That's a cat.

The cat
is playing.

What is that?

That's an elephant.

The elephant
is showering.

What is that?

That's a lion.

The lion
is roaring.

What is that?

That's a giraffe.

The giraffe
is eating.

What is that?

That's a panda.

The panda
is climbing.

Let's learn about Thanksgiving Day.

November

Sunday	Monday	Tuesday	Wednesday	Thursday	Friday	Saturday
1	2	3	4	5	6	7
8	9	10	11	12	13	14
15	16	17	18	19	20	21
22	23	24	25	(26)	27	28
29	30					

Trace the word November
and circle the date.